Seeds of Hope

Living with Mental Health Challenges and Surviving

Nemasa Asetra

Seeds of Hope: Living With Mental Health Challenges and Surviving

Copyright © 2013 by Nemasa Asetra

ISBN 13: 978-1484029602

Printed in USA by Createspace www.createspace.com

Dedication

I dedicate this book, Seeds of Hope: Living With Mental Health Challenges and Surviving to My Peers that I graduated with, who inspired me and touched my life with hope, courage and resilience. I also dedicate this book on mental health recovery to Mr. Terrence Smithers who opened up and shared his experiences with me and my peers. He was an awesome instructor; he lives by what he teaches and is dedicated to what he does to help facilitate and foster a life filled with wellness, recovery, courage, joy, love and peace.

Lastly this book is dedicated to my family, friends and significant others who have supported me in my endeavors throughout the years. Even though I have both adopted and biological family I feel closer to the ones who have reached out to me and brought me into their fold especially my self-created family members of various backgrounds and races.

In Seeds of Hope, the State of Louisiana Certification Course for Peer Support Specialist we gave each other gifts in writing of words, affirmations and notes

Here is the first one I would like to share with everyone: it's from my instructor his gift of teaching has inspired me tremendously.

Nemasa

You have a grace, integrity and resilience to tell your story from a recovery viewpoint that is inspiring. Your skills are natural, kind and effective. It is a pleasure to watch you support others in a way that is comforting, kind and giving. I am so glad you were able to take the challenging years of life and turn them into such an awesome gift for others. Thanks for sharing your story and journey.

Peace....Terrence

Preface

This book is being developed as I sit down in front my pc: computer thinking of a way to tell my recovery story and the journey I will embark upon to get the word out that a life of recovery from mental health challenges and substance use is achievable and doable. Seeds of Hope my peers: helped me to achieve this goal; without them and each of their stories I could not sit here and begin to gather my thoughts.

The purpose of this book is to redefine myself: Nemasa Asetra and tell my story from that of one in recovery. I am one who is no longer speaking, acting or thinking like a victim of circumstances as related to mental health challenges. My life is taking on a new viewpoint shaped and formed around the values and credo of recovery, wellness and support. That is why I must retell and reshape my story and present the new me.

Introduction

Presenting the new Nemasa Asetra, reshaped and redefined; I am learning to put into practice the concepts, ideas and teachings of Recovery Opportunity Center better known as Recovery Innovations Inc... I want to thank you Louisiana, Office of Behavioral Health for my state certification for Peer Support Specialist. I want to share my story of gratitude because of what the Lord has done for me in my life by making me a whole person. I am glad that I found a way to make it to peer support training. I did not think I would make it but I did. I would like to end by saying I am Movin On in the lyrics and words of Rascal Flatts. Because of all my peers I am definitely moving on, emotionally and spiritually. Each of my peers who attended the training shared in my learning processes and they opened up freely. I will always remember that day in my life; it marked a new beginning for me. I am closing the book in my life on playing the victim and I am opening a new book in life, I invite you to take part in my journey as I begin my new chapter in life of redefined recovery from the perspective of a peer support specialist, who was heavily influenced by the viewpoints of Recovery Opportunity Center.

I am filled with joy and I am rejoicing in the Lord for all he has done or me. I no longer ask the question why me Lord. Why did I go rough all of this in my life? I know now I can help someone with my ich experiences in life. Life was not meant to be perfect anyhow. To ly peers who graduated with me I miss all of you already. We bonded nd grew up together quickly and opened up freely each with our own tories of bravery and courage. To my former classmates, I already think f you often and it is just a few days past graduation. I am already eminiscent about my past two week's journey with each of you, my eers. I cherish my gifts of words and affirmations they mean more than naterial possessions and monetary gain. I will think of my peers often as ne Seeds of Hope in recovery who sowed seed into my life and on that ote expect a harvest someday soon and a praise report as I plan to etwork with each of you across the miles and distance that separate each f us throughout the state of Louisiana. **For those who would like to ass a long comments, feedback or anything else I can be contacted t: 504-600-8588 or my email: nasetra@yahoo.com. This work and ll my work is available on Amazon.com**

Hey Nemasa!
think you're terrific. Your're proof that pride in one's heritage and love or all humankind can co-exist in one person.

Warmest Regards,

Jeff

Nemasa
Honesty
Gentle spirit
Inner strength
Self determination
Hopefulness
Thoughtfulness
Kindness
Generous
Ambitious
These are the Strengths I see in you!

~Dani

Nemasa
Kind   Intelligent
Friendly   Hopeful

Have a nice Day

Cliff

Nemasa
    You put out a glow of kindness and have a gentle spirit. I have a great deal of admiration for your commitment your compassion and for never giving up! You are a truly inspirational lady and I feel better off for having met you.   ~ Jeanette

Nemasa

I admire your courage, independence, enthusiasm & strength!
You bring thoughtfulness, kindness & Insight, You carry yourself
With dignity and integrity of a queen indeed.
You are empowered!
Thank you for being a part of my journey

~Kio

Nemasa
Strengths:
        Resourceful, Honest
Generous, Compassionate
Inspirational, Sincere, Strong
Positive, Hopeful, Courageous
Gifts: Genuine Friendship non-judgmental
Caring
                    ~Janet S.

Nemasa

You are very nice, beautiful, courageous, creative, open minded,
informal, and gentle.

                    Tiasha

The Gifts I see in you are that you are Beautiful; the strengths I see in
you are self resilient ~~ You are powerful beyond measure.
                                    Charles B.

Nemasa
The gifts I see in you are: Love Kindness Gentleness
The strengths I see in you are: Independent, Light hearted, Thorough
Honest

Sharon B.

Queen Nemasa
You are talented, determined and resourceful. You are strong resilient
Your gift of Joy is appreciated ~ Bishop O. C.

Nemasa

Ambitious
Adaptable
Intelligent\
Inventive
Polite
Progressive
Social able
Published
Person I am glad the world has you in it. Thanks for being who you are…

John

Nemasa
You are strong and courageous. You have a deep compassion for
helping others. You are selfless.

With Love,

Rachel

Nemasa

You are courageous, ambitious, artistic, non-judgmental, loving woman. I wish you much success in the future.

~ Leslie

Nemasa

The Gifts I see in you: willingness to support others

The strengths I see in your: Helpful, compassionate, generous, and artistic

~Leo

Nemasa

Your determination and courage are great assets. You are going to be a very good Peer Support Specialist.

Nancy

While in class my instructor struck a chord with me when he introduced a song by Rascal Flatts. The song Movin On means so much to me in that it tells my life story in a nutshell when I was unwell and later when I came back strong starting over relocating to Louisiana in 1997.

I'm Movin On

I've dealt with my ghosts and I've faced all my demons
Finally content with a past I regret
I've found you find strength in your moments of weakness
For once I'm at peace with myself
I've been burdened with blame, trapped in the past for too long
I'm movin' on

I've lived in this place and I know all the faces
Each one is different but they're always the same
They mean me no harm but it's time that I face it
They'll never allow me to change
But I never dreamed home would end up where I don't belong
I'm movin' on

I'm movin' on
At last I can see life has been patiently waiting for me
And I know there's no guarantees, but I'm not alone
There comes a time in everyone's life
When all you can see are the years passing by
And I have made up my mind that those days are gone

I sold what I could and packed what I couldn't
Stopped to fill up on my way out of town
I've loved like I should but lived like I shouldn't
I had to lose everything to find out
Maybe forgiveness will find me somewhere down this road
I'm movin' on

I'm movin' on
I'm movin' on

13

Chapter One

For those of you who have asked the question what is a peer support specialist, well simply put, it is a person in mental health or substance use recovery who assist and models a journey of hope, resilience and courage when faced with times of disharmony in one's life.

You might also ask, what is the meaning of recovery? Well according to Recovery Innovations Inc and my instructor who authored the textbooks, it is remembering who you are and using your strengths to become all that you were meant to be. With that in mind there is the concept of Recovery Pathways another term unique to Recovery Innovations Inc and my former instructor, Terrence Smithers. It involves Spirituality, Hope, Recovery Environment, Empowerment, and Choice.

Let's look at (1) Spirituality first, what does it mean to you? It is different for different people for me it is centered on Christ. According to Connecting within and beyond the self; using the force (God) to move forward; seek our own answers to the mystery of the spirit and develop spiritual pathways. (2) Hope is the beginning; it is a thought that things can get better, a feeling of courage with a spark of energy. Hope creates a turning point for me it is getting away from negative forces and celebrating life. Hope means I can have dreams It is a vision of a better future a glass half empty concept focusing on the positive in life. Someone else can hold this hope for us, like a mentor. (3) Recovery Environment use positive language to address yourself and view youself for example: seize to use words like case load, client, patient, drug addict, mentally ill, manipulative, high functioning, low functioning, decompensating, non compliant, convict. Instead use recovery language, person with challenges, person or called us by our name: Nemasa is mine. (4) Empowerment- is the person's own job as a peer support specialist I cannot empower them literally because it is their job to learn how to do for themselves with my assistance as needed without fixing the matter. The person in recovery must take a lead role of his or her own journey in life. The objective is to create a valued role to empower him. Teach good self-advocacy skills that get good results. Promote self-advocacy and give them the lead without taking the power away. (5) Recovery is definitely a choice we must all make, who suffer with some form of mental or substance use challenges. When me make our own choices it helps how we discover who we are. Although making choices for ourselves can be risky we must remember that the person receiving services has a right to these risks. This is the process of learning from our own experiences. And on that note I would say we/ I are the experts of our own choices about our own care. We do best when we choose our services, our service providers, and our service plans.

Chapter Two

I would like to share the definitions and concepts of peer support specialist from the viewpoint of South Carolina Mental Health Dept.

Other Useful Definitions of Peer Support

Self Help

Self Help is the process of relying on one's personal resources and contacts, and not solely the traditional medical community, for information and support about health concerns. With self help, you come to cultivate and rely on your own network of consumer contacts that have successfully gone through many of the same things you are going through. You gain information and support from these people. You come to realize that you have inner strength and unique abilities. You see where others have managed to get through the kinds of situations you find yourself in.

Using self help, you become accustomed to making informed decisions on your own, and not relying on a professional or "higher" authority to understand what is true or possible. A good example is a person who searches out a therapy group on a subject (trauma, as an example) that may not be available at the mental health center and also finds information about trauma in the library or on the Internet.

A person who believes in self help finds peace in following up on their instincts and their heart in matters related to health concerns until they get what they need.

Self Improvement

Self improvement is a broad goal that people in recovery often take on. It refers to personal efforts at making aspects of one's life better, especially if there are things missing in their life that might impede progress toward recovery. For instance, a person might want to work toward going back to school as a way of overcoming feelings of low self esteem. A person might embrace a plan to join an exercise group and to have healthy meals with friends, as a way to raise one's energy levels and take less medication. A self improvement goal is usually not clinical, nor specific to a diagnostic category, but rather holistic in nature and related to life traditionally outside of the mental health service system.

Recovery Role Modeling

Recovery role modeling occurs when a person self identifies as having a mental illness and then demonstrates recovery by sharing their life story. This action reinforces their belief that things have worked out for them, People who tell their recovery stories demonstrate they were able to learn about medications, cope with side effects, stigma, and all the associated disruption that disability brings. Eventually, they are able to successfully pursue and achieve their life's goals. Ike Powell showcases the phenomenon of recovery role modeling in the peer support specialist training segment: "I am a walking miracle!"

Individual Advocacy

Individual advocacy occurs when a person stands up and represents the requests of a person to someone in the system who might not have understood what was being asked or who simply hadn't heard the request. As an example, a client may want to try a certain medication but his case manager doesn't want to make a change. The certified peer support special would work to understand the client's request and the motivation behind it. He would strive to understand why his request is not being honored, and suggest ways to help get the client's request heard. The peer support specialists would also level with the client as to why he is being successful or unsuccessful based on his own experience as a consumer and a staff person. Additional dialogue might focus on what the client might do in the future to be a better self advocate.

Individual Mediation

Individual mediation occurs when the peer support specialist attempts to resolve conflict between the client and another person, with the system or with an outside organization. A good example of this would be a landlord dispute. The certified peer support specialist might also try to access local professional mediation services on behalf of the client. There may be opportunities for the certified peer support specialist to take training in the area of alternative dispute resolution techniques and practices.

Systems Advocacy/Systems Improvement

Systems advocacy/systems improvement occurs when the certified peer support specialist enlists clients to provide input to decision-makers about services for the purposes of program evaluation and making service improvements. Another term for this is *participatory action research* (PAR). It might involve clients surveying other clients, or hosting and participating in focus groups. The outcome of such activity is greater consumer empowerment. Consumers realize that they have the power to have their voice heard and to bring about changes in the system. As an example, the DMH systems are struggling with the backup of clients in emergency waiting rooms. What a peer support specialist would do is to make consumers part of the solution to this situation, rather than the problem. She might host a series of community forums during program hours planned and run for and by consumers to get input from other consumers about how they are managing to avoid using the emergency rooms. This list could then be shared with other consumers and with the broader system of care. They might brainstorm as to how they could help solve this dilemma in their local communities and plan how to take action on their own or with others.

Wellness

Wellness is a term used to describe a level of health in one's life that is positive and holistic - taking into account a mind-body-spirit perspective. The wellness term is counter to the medical community's emphasis on medications and compliance. For mental health consumers, wellness is the goal of all interventions, even if a cure is not possible. Wellness is a concept goal similar to recovery and can also be described as a life journey, a way of being and living happy.

Boundary Setting

Boundary setting is a popular skill with mental health consumers because once they get good at it, it can really help to enhance their relations with other people and to cut down on taking too much on in one's own life. A certified peer support specialist will be trained to host group discussions about boundaries. They can also work one to one with a person on the subject of boundary setting (and breaking) and improving relations with the people in their lives.

Human Appreciation

Human appreciation is an overt demonstration of the appreciation and joy we feel for being alive. This is an egalitarian approach for singing the praises of people. It's celebratory and non-judgmental. It's about helping people to feel good about the here and now.

Adventure

Adventure is a legitimate, therapeutic intervention which takes the client outside of his safety zone and challenges him to survive and interact with people in new and creative ways. Examples of adventure interventions include wilderness camps and ropes courses. At DMH the Palmetto Pride Recovery Retreat experience could be called *adventure therapy*. The outcomes of such approaches include confidence building, increases in perceived control of one's destiny, and hope for the future.

Personal Fulfillment

Personal fulfillment has to do with being able to assign meaning to one's life experience. It's that sense or feeling that you are all that you can be and you are happy with whom you are. Personal fulfillment has much to do with enrichment through relationships with people and one's higher power or God. It has to do with reaching a point of calm and contentment as to one's place and purpose in the world.

The Helper Principle

The Helper Principle occurs when helping other people, one's own burdens in life lift or at least is mitigated. Many people with disabilities report that this is why they volunteer or work within their own disability group. They also report that seeing or helping people better or worse off than themselves helps them to be positive and to appreciate their own situation. By helping in the field they have an opportunity to see people who are modeling a level of recovery which they can aspire to as well. Being involved in a helping field also keeps one abreast of medical advances and basic recovery-related information.

http://www.state.sc.us/dmh/consumer_resources/peer_support/definitions.htm

God will put you at the right place at the right time. He can use your kind words to help someone get back up on their feet again.~ Joel Osteen

Negative Recovery words to take out of your vocabulary as a mental health person in wellness recovery.

Manipulative	replace with survivor or resourceful
High functioning	talented, intelligent
Low functioning	hasn't found his niche that accentuates his talents
Case, client, patient	person receiving services
Frequent flyer	continuing to search for what he needs Seeking recovery and wellness
Unmotivated	not in an environment that's inspiring
A bipolar	Person who has been given a diagnosis of bipolar
Cutter	he sometimes expresses emotional pain harming himself or she creates physical pain to distract herself from emotional pain.

NOTE THE FOLLOWING:

*****A diagnosis presumes that I become my diagnosis and thereby creating hopelessness and what is left is no recovery. ~ Recovery Innovations Inc.

Chapter Three

What now that the load is off my back? Well personally my journey of recovery is about constantly reshaping and redefining myself, pushing out all the negative karma in the world, from my path so that I can function and think. Some negative karma that I am exposed to and unable to get away from like I desire I tune it out. For example, someone in my family and some friends recently told me to stay stuck in my situation of living on social security and subsidized housing their because it was sure thing and I did not want to mess it up. This is their negative language not mine; I want to progress and do better in life. I am pressing forth so God can have his way in my life and use me for his glory honor and praise after all God is my source not social security or subsidized housing don't get me wrong the safety net is needed in times of need but if I can do for myself then why not. I have learned in my past two week journey I must be allowed to make mistakes because from them, the mistakes I will inevitably learn new concepts and ways of thinking. It is like a baby who comes into the world and grows up they must get acclimated into the world and learn from doing, not by always being told what to do. After all, experience is the best teacher with the right role modeling and guidance without fixing things for me.

I like this explanation of recovery from my textbook, it is a quote from Recovery Innovations Inc of a peer's view he says, recovery is a deeply personal unique process changing ones attitude, values, feelings, goals, skills and or roles. It is a way of living a satisfying hopeful and contributing life. Recovery involves the development of new meaning and purpose in one's life as one grows beyond the catastrophic effects of psychiatric disability.

.

Chapter Four

What exactly does a peer support specialist do? I want to begin by quoting what the journey looks like, for a peer support specialist: it is the ability to take one's life experiences and turn pain and suffering into meaningful experiences to transform life into "living hope" for others to model who desire a life of recovery in their journey.

Peers work in a variety of settings throughout the nation and parts of the world. Peers work individually and in groups. They assist with creating goals or service plans like the job of a case manager. They also use recovery tools in the process to foster the desire to conquer challenges.

Another important aspect of PSS: Peer Support Specialist is to assist with helping people develop practical tools, tips and techniques that will help them to create a better day PSS also help with moving people forward on their own recovery journey.

PSS help people create their own self-directed recovery tools. Peers plays a powerful role in empowering people to develop daily plans, identify wellness strategies and create their own self directed recovery tools.

Their own experience with creating these tools is a model of possibility. Later I will explore how this is achieved from the viewpoint of PSS to peers receiving service.

PSS support peers in their decision making. In recovery oriented settings people living with mental health challenges are in charge of making their own decisions.

PSS support others as they make important decisions about their treatment, lifestyle, relationships, and recovery.

PSS set up and sustain self-help groups. It has been demonstrated that peer led, self-help groups increase people's social supports improve their self image and reduce hospital stays.

PSS are uniquely prepared to facilitate these healing groups.

God's plan for your life is so much bigger than your own plan that if God didn't close certain doors it would keep you from the fullness of your destiny.

~Joel Osteen

"Being happy doesn't mean that everything is perfect. It means that you've decided to look beyond the imperfections."

Unknown

happiness

Truth is available
only to those who
have the courage
to question
whatever they
have been taught.

~Annonymous

You'll never be brave
if you don't get hurt.
You'll never learn
if you don't make
mistakes.
You'll never be successful
if you don't encounter
failure.

~ Annonymous

In the process of learning, don't forget to remember who you are, where you have arisen from or rather where you have come from and remember it is so easy for hard times to scar you when they occur and when you forget to remember who you are ~Recovery Innovations Inc. (paraphrased)

In the Thoughts and Words of Gospel Artist Marvin Sapp
He saw the best in me
When everyone else aroundCould only see the
worst in me
Can I tell y'all one more time?
 One more time?
I said he saw the best in me
When everyone else around me Could only see
the worst in me
I wish I had a witness tonight, all I need is one
He saw the best in me
When everyone else around me Could only see
the worst in me
Does anybody have their testimony?
When folks wrote you off Said you would never
make it what did he see?
He saw the best in me
When everyone else around me
When everyone else around could only see the
worst in me
Can I tell you all one more thing?
I just need to tell you one more thing, listen to
this
See, he's mine, and I am his
It doesn't matter what I did

He only sees me for who I am
Does anyone know that tonight?
See he is mine, and I am his
Said it doesn't matter what I did
See, he only sees me for who I am
Help me sing it
Said he is mine(He is mine)Said it doesn't matter
what I did
He only sees me for who I am
He is mine, I am his
It doesn't matter what I did
He only sees me for who I am
I am so glad that he is mine
It doesn't matter what I did
He only sees me for whom I am
He saw the best in me
When everyone else around
Could only see the worst in me
I wish I had a witness tonight
Can I ask ya'll one question?
The question is simply this
What did he see?(He saw the best)
I can't get no help up in here
Because there's some folk in here that people
have wrote you off
Said you would never amount to anything

Said that you would never end up being anywhere
But Myron, tell 'em one more time, what did he see?
He saw the best
When momma said you would never be nothin'
When aunties and uncles said you would never amount to anything
When daddy didn't come home anymore
He didn't look at you and say that you weren't going to make it
God looked at you and what did he see, what did he see?
He saw the best, the best
What did he see?(The best)I said, what did he see?(The best)I said, what did he see?(The best)I said, what did he see?(The best)I said, what did he see?(The best)I said, what did he see?
The Best In Me

Songwriters: SAPP, MARVIN L. / BROWNIE, MATTHEW RICHARD

Never would have made it, never could have made it, without you
I would have lost it all, but now I see how you were there for me

And I can say
Never would have made it,
Never could have made it,
Without you

I would have lost it all,
But now I see how you were there for me and I can say
I'm stronger, I'm wiser, I'm better,
Much better,

When I look back over all you brought me thru.
I can see that you were the one that I held on to
And I never
[Chorus] Never would have made it

Oh I never could have made it
[Chorus] Never could have made it without you

Oh I would have lost it all, oh but now I see how you were there for me

I never
[Chorus] - Never would have made it

No, I never
[Chorus] - Never could have made it without you

I would have lost my mind a long time ago, if it had not been for you.
I am stronger
[Chorus] – I am stronger

I am wiser

[Chorus] – I am wiser

Now I am better
[Chorus] – I am better

So much better
[Chorus] – I am better

I made it thru my storm and my test because you were there to
carry me thru my mess

I am stronger
[Chorus] – I am stronger

I am wiser
[Chorus] – I am wiser

I am better
[Chorus] – I am better

Anybody better
[Chorus] – I am better

I can stand here and tell you, I made it. Anybody out there that you
made it

I am stronger
[Chorus] – I am stronger

I am wiser
[Chorus] – I am wiser

I am better
[Chorus] – I am better

Much better
[Chorus] – I am much better

I made it, I made it, I made it, I made it, I made it, I made it, I made it, I made it

And I never would have made it
[Chorus] Never would have made it

Never could have made it
[Chorus] Never could have made it without you

I would have lost my mind, I would have gave up, but you were
right there, you were right there

I never
[Chorus] Never would have made it

Oh I never
[Chorus] - I never could have made it without you.

Someone need to testify next to them and tell them I am stronger,
I am wiser,
I am better, much better.
When I look back over what he brought me thru.
I realize that I made it because I had you to hold on to,
Now I am stronger, now I am wiser,
I am better, so much better.
I made it.
Is there anybody in this house other than me that can declare that
you made it.
Tell your neighbor, never would have made it.
Never would have made it.
Never could have made it.
Never could have made it without you.
Never would have made it.
Never would have made it.
Never could have made it.
Never could have made it without you

Never Would Have Made It lyrics

A Credo of Support

Read by People with Disabilities

Read by a Narrator

Throughout history, people with physical and mental disabilities have been abandoned at birth, banished from society, used as court jesters, drowned and burned during The Inquisition, gassed in Nazi Germany, and still continue to be segregated, institutionalized, tortured in the name of behavior management, abused, raped, euthanized, and murdered.

Now, for the first time, people with disabilities are taking their rightful place as fully contributing citizens.

The danger is that we will respond with remediation and benevolence rather than equity and respect. And so, we offer you:

A Credo for Support

Do not see my disability as the problem.
Recognize that my disability is an attribute.

Do not see my disability as a deficit.
It is you who see me as deviant and helpless.

Do not try to fix me because I am not broken.
Support me. I can make my contribution to the community in my own way.

Do not see me as your client.
I am your fellow citizen.

See me as your neighbor.
Remember, none of us can be self-sufficient.

Do not try to modify my behavior. Be still & listen. What you
define as inappropriate may be my attempt to communicate with
you in the only way I can.

Do not try to change me, you have no right.
Help me learn what I want to know.

Do not hide your uncertainty behind "professional" distance.
Be a person who listens and does not take my struggle away from
me by trying to make it all better. Do not use theories and
strategies on me.
Be with me.
And when we struggle with each other let that give use to self-
reflection.

Do not try to control me. I have a right to my power as a person.
What you call non-compliance or manipulation may actually be the
only way I can exert some control over my life.

Do not teach me to be obedient, submissive and polite.
I need to feel entitled to say No if I am to protect myself.

Do not be charitable towards me.
The last thing the world needs is another Jerry Lewis.

Do not try to be my friend. I deserve more than that.
Get to know me, we may become friends.

Do not help me, even if it does make you feel good.
Ask me if I need your help.
Let me show you how you can assist me.

Do not admire me.
A desire to live a full life does not warrant adoration.
Respect me, for respect presumes equality.

Do not tell, correct, and lead.
Listen, support, and follow.

Do not work on me.
Work with me!

In Memory of <u>Tracy Latimore</u>
Written by Norman Kunc and Emma Van der Klift
Copyright 1995 Norman Kunc & Emma Van der Klift

Chapter Five

The typical day in the life of a Peer Support Specialist, is not so typical for the majority of PSS. Their day includes running a support group in the AM, early morning and later documenting their peers progress while doing paperwork for a few hours. Later, they may meet with 3 or 4 peers over the course of the afternoon.

The following day may include visiting some peers at home, running a peer led artist group and later doing more paperwork. A Peer Support Specialist has many roles in many different settings.

Some peer support specialist work part-time a few hours a week, while others work on a volunteer basis. Others work fulltime holding positions as supervisors or leaders of teams of other Peer Support Specialist.

Chapter Six

Where do Certified Peer Support Specialist Work? Typically they offer services in addition to the professional care someone receives. They work everywhere that people are dealing with mental health challenges. **For example, you will find Peer Support Specialist in the community run behavioral health centers, public or private mental health agencies, Jails, Homeless Shelters, Hospitals, and Day Treatment Programs.**

Most often PSS work as paid employees. Some however, offer services as a volunteer like I intend to do, at a local agency in my community.

Chapter Seven

Where am I headed in life now? Honestly I am in an exploration mode and I am not for sure, currently I am on the New Orleans, LA Behavioral Health Interagency Council Committee and I am very honored to be selected by both my peers and the policy makers. I will be using my newly acquired skills as a platform of expression for my peers and myself. In addition I will be volunteering at a local agency as a Peer Mentor and helping to shape and redefine recovery language etc. Words cannot express my joy and excitement for wellness recovery and resiliency in mental health for both me and my peers. Please come along for the ride as I keep you informed of my progress as well as the latest news updates in peer support training from the perspective of a Certified Peer Support Specialist. Thank you for checking out my recovery story it is a new beginning for me. As I follow in the footsteps of the Official Pioneer, Toni Bonvillon in Peer Support for the state of Louisiana I say it like that because when I lived and worked at an independent living facility in Baton Rouge, LA Margaret Chaney had put in place her version of Peer Support Specialist that was back in 1998 and it was very effective. On that note I would just like to say that peer support specialist got a kick off in the field after Hurricane Katrina around year 2005 or so. At that time the official Peer Support Specialist was Toni Bonvillon she was at my graduation telling her story and how she developed a curriculum. It is heroic and very outstanding her work is greatly appreciated.

Tips on How to Speak to Someone or View Someone in Recovery

1. Use Reflection ie. Repeat back to them what you heard them say.
2. Relate to them with empathy ie. Recall a time when you shared a similar experience and show you care.
3. Validate their strengths for example you can let them know they are very brave or courageous for bringing their concern in the open and for opening up to you or me the peer.
4. Then ask permission to discuss it, the concern with them ex. would you like to discuss your feelings about this matter.
5. Always ask Open Ended Questions

~ Recovery Innovations Inc.

My Recovery Story

My Journey in the mental health system began in 1989 when I had my first mental health challenge. I experienced hearing and seeing things no one else saw or heard. I was afraid and confused about what was occurring in my life. I was opposed to the medication because it made me feel like a zombie. Years passed and in 1993 I found a psychiatrist I could trust. I became compliant with one medication but at the time I needed another for depression however I was not having it because I felt like it was going to do me harm and have me stifled even more than I already was. At the time I was in college doing well working on a bachelors' in Africana Studies. I did well holding my own looking forward to teaching as a college professor as I had been impressed by many of my instructors and inspired. However a few years would pass and my adopted mom would have her first stroke and at the time I had to do the forbidden which was to place her in a convalescing home as a result she did not want to be there and she had another stroke in the meantime I had a major case of depression with psychiatric symptoms such as mania, voices, visions and hallucinations. While my mom lay dying and on life support I had to be hospitalized in a psychiatric facility I stayed there until after the funeral. In the meantime, my family planned the funeral and afterwards everything spiraled down. My family came and got me for the funeral afterwards I had to return to the hospital for observation. When the next day arrived I had made preparation to stay at a friend's group home where I was exploited and taken advantaged of. Meantime another classmate from college offered me to stay with her mom in the garage apartment. At the time, my fate in life was uncertain; as time progressed I got sick and experienced a major mental health challenge, on campus I got evicted from my housing. And I ended up staying in a motel. Later I stopped taking my medication and began acting out living in a realm of utter confusion with the following psychiatric symptoms: hearing voices, seeing visions and hallucinating. A time came when I acted out on a daily basis, one day the police came and kindly took me to the hospital I got treatment while there and a supply of medication when I came to myself I realized I was ill and needed help, I asked my adopted dad for help he and his wife agreed to it. Later, I traveled on Amtrak with a one way ticket to Franklin, La and when I arrived I was met with resistance. I ended up going in the hospital and when got well and a renewed sense of understanding and reasoning I asked to go to a group home. I traveled on the Greyhound to Baton Rouge, LA I arrived at Ms. Alvira Williams and Mr.

Williams they picked me up. I did not stay there long and later I traveled on my journey to Phoenix Personal Care Services Inc, where Margaret Chaney was the director and owner. At the time it was called St Dyphna it was an independent living facility I stayed there from 1997 to 1999 afterwards I did the forbidden again and got involved with her son. She said it was all in my mind and had me to leave the facility. From there I went back to Alvira Williams and later to the housing development of Baton Rouge I stopped taking my medication. One day I acted out of character and hit someone who hit me first and ended up in East Baton Rouge Parish Jail. While there I was mistreated. I acted out in defense of myself and it caused my stay to be a little longer than it should have been. Meanwhile I had to go to Forensics in Jackson, LA when I got well I returned to EBR Parish Jail and later I went through the court system I met with a public defender that encouraged me to not react to people next time, to take my medication and to think before responding. After I went to court I was told all charges would be dropped I had to secure somewhere to stay and so I did I was placed in Synergy Behavioral Health of Baton Rouge, LA independent living program that was in 2000, in 2001 I relocated to New Orleans,L A and I had some good times, rough times being homeless but never in the streets after Hurricane Katrina I stayed with a friend and their family time progressed upon the urging

61

of the friends family I moved out which was short lived. My job at Ochsner Hospital was famous for sending people home early or canceling a shift. Not only that but I later got on my feet again and began to do well then one day I injured myself at work I had to deal with the workers compensation adjuster who cared more about saving Ochsner and her company money as a result I did not get the care I needed in the meantime I had a mental health challenge I decided one day to stop taking my medication it was not helping me in the meantime I became untrusting of others and I said and did things inappropriately for which I was not proud of and had to apologize and ask forgiveness. Later I moved out of my cheap rented apartment because the rent was going up I decided to stay at a hotel and when I did I ran out of money and asked my adopted dad to come get me his response was to go to a shelter and that was it. I ended up going to Jefferson parish lock up for 8 hours I asked my dad again to come get me he did not so later after staying outside in front the jail for a few nights I finally realized I had money on my atm card I went to the doctor to get my blood pressure treated and they sent me on my way. I ended up back in New Orleans, LA and I was given a voucher for a taxi that took me to the Salvation Army and later I went to Franklin where my family had me hospitalized. Next stage of my journey took me to Morgan City, LA where I stayed in the hospital over a month I decided on the group home in Marksville, LA called Cutting Edge, while there I protested and demanded better care and service instead I got arrested for disturbing the peace charges. I was then sent to Avoyelles Parish Correctional Facility and while there I was mistreated. I was not afraid but I felt intimidated because I was in a prison system and I acted out the whole time I was there later I was sent to a hospital in Breaux Bridge, LA afterwards I decided on a group home in Opelousas I did not like it there as a result I decided to come back to New Orleans and I got as close as I could. My next journey brought me to Wren Way Ladies at the South Eastern Louisiana Psychiatric Hospital Facility. It was too restricted and the staff seemed to think they had job security and that I could stay there forever and move into the apartments but I was not having it, there were too many rules and criteria so I decided to take a taxi back to New Orleans, LA once my worker's comp was restored I stayed in a hotel got back with my friend and later I rented a duplex and afterwards things were rocky as life is always rocky but my journey has led to sharing my story with others to help and encourage them. Today I am an author of more than one autobiography I have been encouraged to write my story by clergy and so I have, I have revised it and made changes to my book to make it more presentable and attractive by trial and error. Lastly I would like to say that I did not understand my journey and wished it had not happen to me but it has led to new opportunities despite circumstances I am an advocate, activist and a member of the New Orleans Behavioral Health Interagency Council Committee. I am also certified as a NAMI Smart Advocate and in Suicide Prevention I am very proud and happy and looking forward to serving my peers while helping as well as sharing my experiences after all my story like all stories of hope are unique and all stories of struggle to strength are meant to touch someone's life; it is not about me but it is hope inspiration, joy, love and peace.

Peace and Blessings

Nemasa Asetra

Biography

Nemasa Asetra was born in 1966 she was born to Mildred Emerson Thomas and given to Vera Johnson Hartman and Matthew Hartman her adopted parents. She is a native of Los Angeles, CA who currently resides in New Orleans, LA the city that is known for its authentic Nawlins culture of good festivals, art, music and cuisines. Nemasa has resided in New Orleans since 2002 and loves to call Nawlins home. She is new to the concepts of recovery, wellness and resilience and hopes to share her story with her peers and anyone interested in learning about what a peer support specialist is and what a day in the life of a certified peer specialist is like. Her interest is reading, writing, research and surfing the internet including spending time on social network sites like Facebook communicating with friends and family members across the miles that separate us.

Rhema Word
Accept what God allowed, and accept what man cannot change. Keep moving forward and keep looking ahead.
~ Prophetess Rosie Burney Finley

Challenge yourself to never give up. Even if you have days when you're not very successful, keep believing. I think it makes the devil furious when we keep saying I believe that God is working and I am free.

~ Joyce Meyer

Take off the "failure," "guilty," "condemned" labels and put on something new: "redeemed, restored, forgiven, new beginning."

~Joel Osteen

Those who walk in GREATNESS & success aren't because they have everything going for them but because they refuse to quit & give up on their dream!

~ Paula White

Impossible is a big word thrown around by small men who find it easier to live in the world they've been given than to explode the power they have to change it. Impossible is not a fact, it's an opinion. Impossible is not a declaration: It's a dare Impossible is potential! Impossible is temporary.

~ Addidas

If you don't chase your dreams you will never reach your destiny
~ Warriors of Black Consciousness

Invest in the
human soul.
Who knows,
it might be a
diamond in the
rough.

~ Mary McLeod Bethune

"WE'VE GOT TO LIVE, NO MATTER HOW MANY SKIES HAVE FALLEN"

DH LAWRENCE

Sometimes you have to fall from the mountains to realize what you're fighting for. Obstacles are placed in our way to see if what we want is worth fighting for. From every wound, there's a scar, and every scar tells a story. A story that says, "I was deeply wounded but I survived."

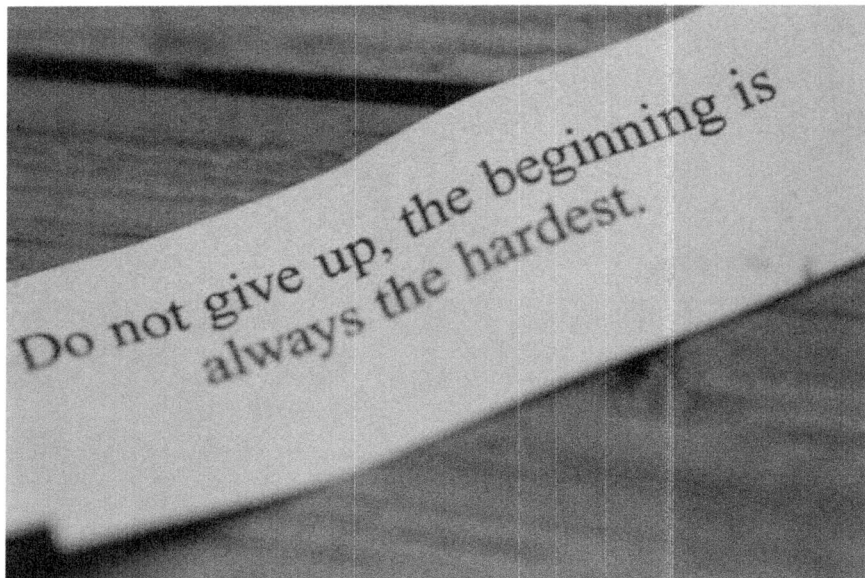

Do not give up, the beginning is always the hardest.

GOD
Always Has Something For You

A Key For Every Problem
A Light For Every Shadow
A Relief For Every Sorrow
A Plan For Every Tomorrow

don't waste your
time looking back
for what you've lost

MOVE ON

for life wasn't meant to
be traveled backwards

Two things define you.
Your patience when you have nothing, and your attitude when you have everything.

rawforbeauty.com

STOP
WAITING
FOR
THINGS
TO
HAPPEN
GO
OUT
AND
MAKE
THEM
HAPPEN

Photos of my seeds of Hope Graduation

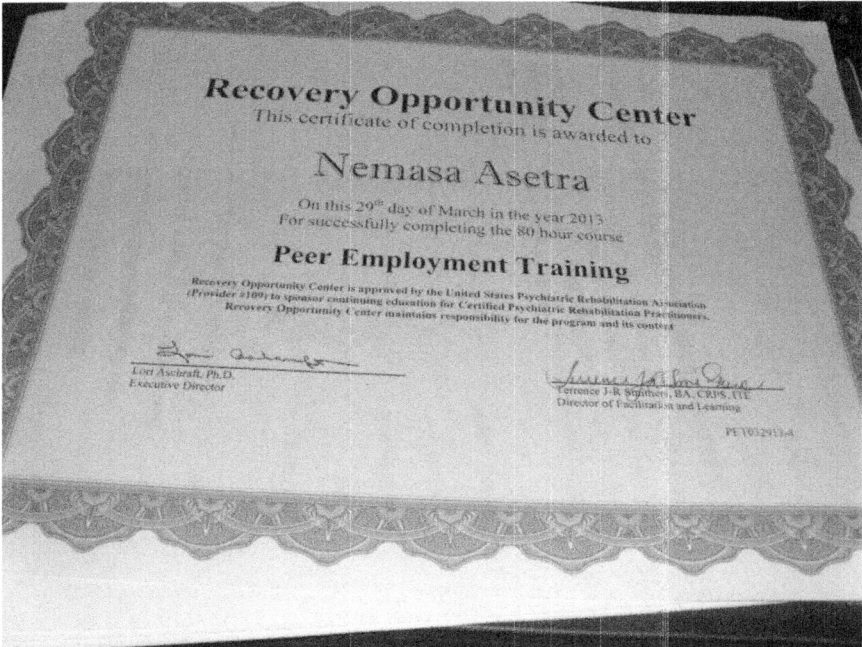

Recovery Opportunity Center

This certificate of completion is awarded to

Nemasa Asetra

On this 29th day of March in the year 2013
For successfully completing the 80 hour course

Peer Employment Training

Recovery Opportunity Center is approved by the United States Psychiatric Rehabilitation Association
(Provider #109) to sponsor continuing education for Certified Psychiatric Rehabilitation Practitioners.
Recovery Opportunity Center maintains responsibility for the program and its content

Lori Ashcraft, Ph.D.
Executive Director

Terrence J-R Stithers, BA, CRPS, CIE
Director of Facilitation and Learning

PET032913-4

Recovery Opportunity Center
Recovery Innovations, Inc.
Peer Employment Training Grade Sheet
New Orleans Seeds of Hope – March 18-29, 2013

Name: _Yenasa Asutra_

Mid-Term: _98_

Final: _95_

Participation: _100_

Attendance: _100_

Course Grade: _97.2A_

Thank you for allowing me this opportunity to share this journey wit
you. It has been my honor to be with you as you discover, uncove
develop and nurture the skills you can now carry forward to promote
hope and reality of recovery in the lives of others.

Be kinder than necessary for everyone you meet is facing some kind of challe

Congratulations Graduates!

Seeds of Hope

Peer Employment Training

March 29, 2013

When the enemy tells you, "You're just average, ordinary, less than," reject those lies and remember, "You are an overcomer, more than a conqueror." God has given you seeds of greatness. ~ Joel Osteen

Made in the USA
Las Vegas, NV
20 December 2022

63584573R00049